Alma Flor Ada　•　F. Isabel Campoy

Voices

Luis Valdez

Judith Francisca Baca

Carlos Juan Finlay

Illustrated by Pablo Rulfo, Isaac Hernández, and Beatriz Rodríguez

ALFAGUARA

YOUNG READERS
SANTILLANA

Originally published in Spanish as *Voces*

Art Director: Felipe Dávalos
Design: Petra Ediciones
Editor: Norman Duarte

Cover: Felipe Dávalos

Santillana USA Publishing Company, Inc.
2105 NW 86th Avenue
Miami, FL 33122

Biography C: *Voices*

ISBN: 1-58105-572-2

The authors gratefully acknowledge the editorial assistance of Rosa Zubizarreta.

ILLUSTRATORS
ISAAC HERNÁNDEZ: pp. 17-22
BEATRIZ RODRÍGUEZ: pp. 23-32
PABLO RULFO: pp. 6-14

Printed in Colombia
Panamericana Formas e Impresos S.A.

ACKNOWLEDGEMENTS

Page 5 / Luis Valdez. Photo provided by El Teatro Campesino, San Juan Bautista, California.
Page 7 / Children in a migrant worker camp, 1959. Copyright © AP / Wide World Photos.
Page 7 / Migrant workers in a California farm, 1964. Copyright © AP / Wide World Photos.
Pages 8-9 / Migrant worker harvesting tomatoes in California, 1978. Copyright © AP / Wide World Photos.
Page 11 / Ventriloquist Jerry Mahoney. Copyright © 1988 Capital Cities / ABC, Inc. / The Everett Collection.
Page 13 / Luis Valdez. Copyright © 1981 Universal City Studios Inc. / The Everett Collection.
Page 13 / César Chávez and striking farmworkers, 1966. Copyright © George Ballis / Take Stock / The Everett Collection.
Page 15 / Photo by Gia Roland provided by Judith F. Baca.
Page 16 / Judith F. Baca, *Tres generaciones (Three Generations)*. Copyright © Judith F. Baca / Social and Public Arts Resource Center (SPARC), Venice, California.
Page 17 / Judith F. Baca, *Hitting the Wall: Women of the Marathon,* 1984. Copyright © Judith F. Baca / Social and Public Arts Resource Center (SPARC), Venice, California.
Page 19 / Judith F. Baca at age six, Pacoima, California. Photo provided by Judith F. Baca / Social and Public Arts Resource Center (SPARC), Venice, California.
Page 19 / Judith F. Baca at her graduation from Alemany High School, 1964. Photo provided by Judith F. Baca / Social and Public Arts Resource Center (SPARC), Venice, California.
Pages 20-21 / Judith F. Baca, "Triumph of the Heart," 1989. Panel from *World Wall: A Vision of the Future Without Fear.* Copyright © Judith Baca / Social and Public Arts Resource Center (SPARC), Venice, California.
Page 20 / Mural by Diego Rivera, Teatro de los Insurgentes, Mexico City. Photo by Marco / Ask Images / The Viesti Collection.
Page 21 / José Clemente Orozco, *La trinchera (The Trench),* 1923-27. Escuela Nacional Preparatoria San Ildefonso, Mexico City. Copyright © Clemente Orozco Valladares. Reproduction authorized by the Instituto Nacional de Bellas Artes y Literatura, Mexico City, and the Fundación José Clemente Orozco, Guadalajara, Jalisco.
Page 22 / Judith F. Baca, "Balance," 1990. Panel from *World Wall: A Vision of the Future Without Fear.* Copyright © Judith F. Baca / Social and Public Arts Resource Center (SPARC), Venice, California.
Page 31 / Havana Harbor, 1904. Cuban Heritage Collection, Otto G. Richter Library, University of Miami, Coral Gables, Florida.
Page 31 / The restaurant Gran París, Havana, c. 1900. Cuban Heritage Collection, Otto G. Richter Library, University of Miami, Coral Gables, Florida.

Contents

To Barbara, Carol, and Mikey,
from Tanglewood, with love.

To Peg Doherty,
an exemplary life.

Luis Valdez

Frank and Armida Valdez lived in Arizona. One day, they moved to California. They were looking for a better life. They bought a farm near Delano, California. Their son Luis was born there on June 26, 1940. Luis was the second of ten children.

The Valdez family was always bound by their love for each other.

When Luis was still young,
his parents lost the farm.
They started working as migrant farm workers.

Migrant farm workers
go from field to field looking for work.
They pick fruits and other crops.

Migrant workers
and their families
live in camps
with very few comforts.

Because they needed to be on the move, the children had to change schools often. They had to get to know a new teacher each time.

It was sad to leave their friends behind. Yet Luis always took the opportunity to learn something new every time they moved.

In one of his schools, the teacher announced that they were going to rehearse a play. Luis was given a part in the play. He had never done any acting before. He didn't know what to expect, but as the rehearsals got underway, he was delighted.

Theater allows us to become our dreams.

But one week before opening night, his family told Luis that they would be moving again.

That was really painful for Luis.
He had wanted so much to be in the play!
But then he decided to create his own theater in his grandfather's garage.

His brothers and sisters enjoyed being his audience. He created puppets and made up stories. And those he could take with him wherever he went.

When he had to pick crops in the fields alongside his parents, he would think about his characters:
What will they say?
How will they dress?
How will they move?

When Luis was in high school, a friend gave him a ventriloquist's dummy.

Luis practiced talking with his mouth closed.
He rehearsed long dialogs with his dummy in front of a microphone.

Soon he began to be known in San José, California,
as a performer.

One day a TV station called him.
They wanted him to perform with his dummy on
a bilingual program.

They paid him five dollars for each show.
It was 1956. Luis was sixteen years old.

The ventriloquist Jerry Mahoney
and his dummies were very well
known. Luis Valdez
often saw them on television.

His interest in theater did not keep Luis from studying. On the contrary, Luis knew that he could not go far without an education.

He studied math and science. When he finished high school, he received a scholarship to study at San José State College.

Theater became popular thanks to radio.

He went to college with the idea of studying science, but then he realized that he could study literature and devote his time to theater and writing movie scripts.

Luis founded the *Teatro Campesino* (Farm Workers' Theater) to perform plays about the life of Latinos in California. Many of the original actors were farm workers.

The stage helps the stories seem real.

Luis now works in the movies, too. He wrote the scripts for *Zoot Suit* and *La Bamba*. He is also a director.

Today this child of farm workers is an important figure in the world of stage and screen.

Luis Valdez's life teaches us to hold on to our dreams.

Luis Valdez directed the film *Zoot Suit* in 1981. He was also the scriptwriter.

Judith Francisca Baca

Judith Francisca was a happy child.

She was the center of attention for three women: her mother, her grandmother, and her aunt.

She lived with them until she was five years old.

Judith painted herself as a child and as a young artist accompanied by her mother Ortencia and her grandmother Francisca.

Judith also had another aunt who played with her as though she were a little girl too.

The relationship among these five women was strong, positive, and loving.

Surrounded by them, Judith learned to be strong, to be sure of herself, and to feel love and compassion for others.

In the city of Los Angeles there are many murals. This mural by Judith Baca, entitled *Hitting the Wall: Women of the Marathon,* is at the entrance of a freeway that leads downtown.

At the age of six, Judith went to live with her mother and her mother's new husband in Pacoima, California.

When she went to her new school, the teacher did not speak Spanish. So she sent Judith to a corner and told her to draw while she taught the other students.

Judith found that her colored pencils were her best friends.

Judith was very much alone in school.

Her passion for painting grew.

When she finished high school, Judith wanted to go to college and learn more about art.

And she did. After finishing her university degree, Judith conceived a beautiful project. She wanted to work with teenagers of different cultural backgrounds in order to paint a great mural.

Judith always remembered the strength that she derived from her grandmother's hands and from her family. She wanted to transmit this sense of security to young people.

Before beginning a project, Judith Francisca asked the members of her team to hold hands. They reflected on the idea that, together, their hands would achieve the goal.

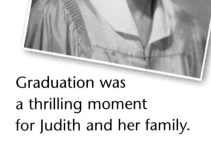

Judith at six.

Graduation was a thrilling moment for Judith and her family.

This mural by Diego Rivera is found on Insurgentes Avenue in Mexico City.

The most important moment in Judith's career was when she discovered the great Mexican muralists: José Clemente Orozco, Diego Rivera, and David Alfaro Siqueiros.

After she saw photographs of their work, she decided to go to Mexico to see the murals.

And she became a muralist herself.

Triumph of the Heart is one panel of the mural *World Wall: A Vision of the Future Without Fear* by Judith F. Baca

The city government of Los Angeles understood Judith's great project and gave her everything she needed to create over two hundred multicultural murals throughout the city.

Her largest project was the mural for *Great Wall* in the San Fernando Valley. It is half a mile long.

Baca has created another monumental mural entitled *World Wall: A Vision of the Future Without Fear*. This mural, which has been shown in Moscow and several other places around the world, expresses her feelings about world peace.

This mural by José Clemente Orozco can be found in the San Ildefonso National School in Mexico City.

This panel from Baca's mural, *World Wall: A Vision of the Future Without Fear*, is entitled *Balance*. It has been exhibited in many countries.

Judith Francisca Baca's life and work reflect her faith in the family and her hope for a common willingness to create peace and justice among people.

Carlos Juan Finlay

Carlos Juan Finlay wanted to be a doctor.
He wanted to cure sick people.
His father was a doctor.

Carlos Juan was born in the city of Camagüey
in Cuba. His parents were not from Cuba. His
father came from Scotland and his mother came
from France. He was proud to be a Cuban.

Carlos Juan was a very curious boy.
His favorite question was "Why?"
He wanted to learn the mysteries of nature.
He wanted to know about animals, plants,
and life in general.

When he was eleven years old, he was sent to France to study.

Two years later, Carlos Juan became very sick. It was a serious illness. Many doctors helped to save his life. He went back to Cuba. But he had to re-learn how to speak.

Carlos Juan did not die, but he was never able to talk as he had before his illness. He had a speech impediment for the rest of his life. This meant that he could not pronounce words clearly.

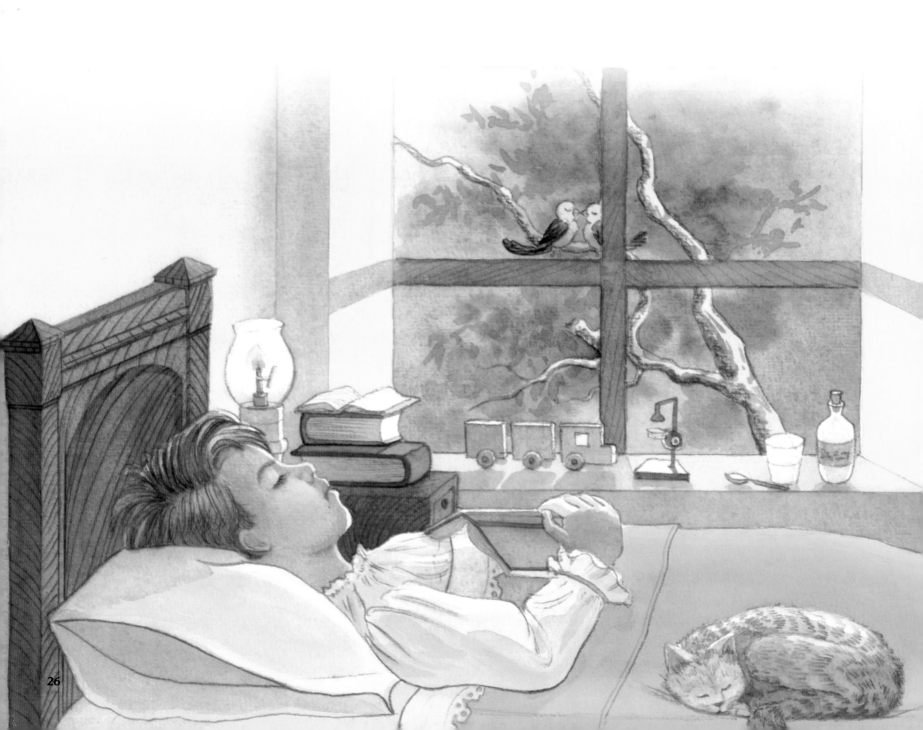

Carlos Juan finished his medical studies
at the age of twenty-two. He had studied
in France, Germany, the United States,
and Cuba.

When he was in Cuba again, he became
concerned about a disease that caused the deaths
of many of his patients. Their skin would turn
yellow. This is why it was called yellow fever.

Nobody knew the cause of yellow fever. Some
doctors said it was the heat. Others said that it
was the lack of cleanliness. Others believed that
it was spread by patients' clothing.

Carlos Juan noticed that in the summer,
when ponds were swarming with mosquitoes,
there were more patients with yellow fever.

So he decided to observe the mosquitoes.
Could they be the cause of this illness?

Finlay discovered that if a mosquito bit someone who was sick, and then bit someone who wasn't sick, the healthy person became ill with yellow fever.

Carlos Finlay tried to explain his discovery to other doctors.

He went to Washington.
He spoke at a big medical convention.
But no one paid any attention to what he had to say. They laughed at his idea. Nobody respected him because of his speech impediment.

He was called the Mosquito Doctor.

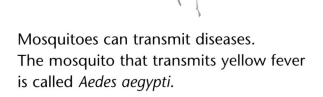

Mosquitoes can transmit diseases.
The mosquito that transmits yellow fever is called *Aedes aegypti*.

Finlay bred his own mosquitoes to study them.

Many years passed. A group of doctors from the United States went to Cuba. They wanted to study yellow fever. The head of the study team was Dr. Walter Reed. Finlay went to visit them.

The Cuban doctor with a white beard explained his idea. At first, they paid little attention to Finlay.

But Dr. Reed decided to listen to Finlay. The Cuban doctor gave Dr. Reed the information he had collected for thirty years. He even gave him the mosquitoes he had bred.

The American doctors decided to test the idea.

One courageous doctor named Dr. James Carroll allowed himself to be bitten by a mosquito.

The mosquito had bitten a person with yellow fever before that.

Dr. Carroll became sick. Finlay's idea was correct!

Havana Harbor at the beginning of the twentieth century.

Thanks to Finlay,
a war against mosquitoes was declared.

In Cuba and in other tropical countries where there are lots of mosquitoes, people covered stagnant water with a layer of oil.

The mosquitoes disappeared.
Yellow fever disappeared.
People stopped getting sick.
People stopped dying.

Gran Paris Restaurant in Havana at the beginning of the twentieth century.

Dr. Walter Reed brought the results of his research to the United States.
He received many honors for this work.

He was called the "discoverer of yellow fever."

Nobody remembered Finlay, who died without so much as a thank you from anyone.

Forty years after his death, his contributions to medical research were finally recognized.